# MOTORCYCLE HAIKU 5

## Lobo Solitario continues exploring America through Black and White Images

### MARK FARGO

# Haiku

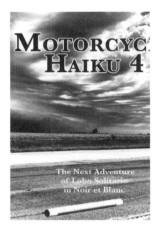
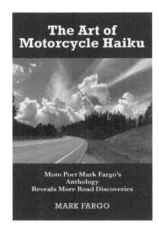
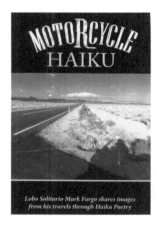

# MOTORCYCLE HAIKU 5

## MARK FARGO

Copyright © 2024

All rights reserved, including the reproduction in whole or in part in any form without the written consent of the author.

ISBN: 978-1-965407-5-4-7 (paper back)
ISBN: 978-1-965407-5-4-7 (ebook)

Book Design by Blue Jay Ink
Ojai, California
bluejayink.com

Published in the United States by
Lone Wolf Prints in association with Creative Book Writers

markfargo.com

"Color photography is like your skin, you can change its appearance, but Black and White photography is like your bones and marrow, it's the base of life."

– Anonymous

# Foreward

I did an experiment with this 5th book of Mark's Motorcycle Haiku series. Like previous anthologies, this one is illustrated by both poetry and photos that offer abounding insight into the places and spaces of our great land. My experiment... I did not read a thing; not haiku, not tanka, not captions... not even page numbers! I only reflected on the black and white images for seconds before turning the page, and I did this in one session. It was like that trick of animation, a flip-book of images that seems to move as quickly as a Yamaha Tenere.

Then, in the second phase of my inquiry, I used an index card to block the photos, leaving only the text. I read and reflected happily on my method, concluding that both words and images were kin and that they collided amicably somewhere in that part of my brain that draws meaning from both the word and from the image.

This volume, Mark's 5th, recalls the progression of his wanderlust starting with grueling junkets on a BMW scooter, a flip-phone, an IPad, and a body 10 years younger that had not yet been over 200,000 miles down the roads of America, and back again.

So, experiment as you will, but realize that the soul of the poet and the soul of the rider grow deeper with each new book of verse and image. Mark's genre is unique and deserves to be consumed in unique ways; unique as Mark's way of experiencing America.

Gary Delanoeye
(www.garydelanoeye.com)

## Bones and Marrow

Some people accuse motorcyclists as being a touch too attached to their ride, spending more time polishing chrome or trying to get every speck of dirt from the paint off than spending time with your family. I don't want to get to the point of obsession to the point of no return. Ha. I'm no exception, but I don't ignore my family and friends because I don't have time for them. I'm not the encyclopedia of knowledge regarding the history of motorcycles, what's the latest trend nor having in depth knowledge of all the makes and models, but I am loyal to Yamaha products as they have, with just routine maintenance and putting premium gasoline into the tank, a top tier ride that's dependable and fun to ride. As we dive into book five of my Motorcycle Haiku travels, I will always be a Yamaha rider. I know there are plenty of excellent choices on the market, but as the old saying goes, "If it ain't broke, don't fix it" and Yamahas don't break.

# Dedication

A Tanka is a thirty-one 5-7-5-7-7 syllable format genre of Japanese poetry that addresses sorrow or loss. I honor those who have left us, saddened by their passing. The fourth one, Fallout, is in regard to my home state of California and its latest environmental challenges that are currently in progress.

## Last Pitch

Last start not scheduled
liked everybody he met
he loved his Cubbies
battled sunrises and sunsets
cancer comes but never leaves

## Mom #2

Food always around
stomping down the hall yelling
card games with the girls
safe haven for me tough times
Lizzy favorite fur-ball

## Last Christmas

Loved by everyone
plastered drywall union man
Nora his life mate
his face always smiling
the world has lost a great soul

## Fallout

More rains more flooding
no longer just earthquakes fires
mudslides and mayhem
streets becoming tire graveyards
rubber peeling off.

## Favorite Son

Floor length dreadlocks coat
you were cautious at the start
we earned your respect
final moments deep abyss
joyful snapshots ease our pain

## Survivor

Southern Italian
his father no fun too strict
beatings were normal
harsh life no love nor future
America saved your life

## CONSTANT COMPANION

Hand painted 6.1 gallon gas tank gathers lots of attention and compliments. There are thousand of Lobo's out there like me.

# Introduction

I was watching an old rerun of California Gold, that great show with that gentle giant ex-marine from Gallatin, Tennessee, the personable Huell Houser. He delivered yet another folksy episode of the hidden gems of the greatest state in the union, California, and its world renown state flower, the golden poppy, as well as the super wildflower blooms, found almost statewide when the weather assists, in a short but spectacular season. As a seasoned solo rider, my life on two wheels is a privileged gem that I have not taken for granted, and I will always feel that California is still the best place to ride year-round in the United States.

Since I began my new life in 2013, motorcycling all across the country in my late fifties, I always thought I could replace Houser after he passed in 2013, with a new, expanded version of the show, America on Two Wheels. Granted it was a pipe dream of mine as it was selfish of me to think of replacing a legend so quickly with an unknown, just starting out, soon to be retired high school teacher with a Beatnik poetry background, a senior citizen motorcyclist who didn't start writing haiku poetry until it was recommended by two Japanese exchange students during my last year of teaching in 2016. This is a huge, massive run on sentence. Please forgive me. Ha.

These two female students, likely here to work on their English, as they had already completed most of our country's graduation requirements by the end of their junior year in Japan, choose a Title I school in an almost ninety percent Hispanic demographic in Oxnard California as their choice for acquiring the most spoken language in the world. I ended up as the advisor for Club Japanese, which was largely attended by other members of the student body. The club was very successful, and we even ended up in Little Tokyo in Los Angeles for a field trip. I was referred to as Fargosan by these two charming exchange students. Japanese students respect their teachers. To honor them in my path to Haiku Heaven, I personalized my license plate to say LOBOSAN, a morph of wolf, with the other half honoring my students' respect for teachers. (Half Japanese).

They convinced me that Haiku was the way to capture my whimsical and yet very dramatic photography, especially now that I'm mostly producing black and white chapbooks. Kind of restrictive I thought, but I'm a very adaptable person so let's give it a try. My first book, Motorcycle Haiku, was first published in 2017. A friend and neighbor, Frank Boros, who has since tragically passed, pulled out a standard 8 by 11 inch lined notebook paper, folded it in half, and suggested that I start a series of chapbooks recording my journeys. That 5-inch by 8-inch chapbook was the perfect size for my format and an easy travel book for some of my followers. Some had them on plane flights and mentioned to me it was the perfect escape read on their flight.

I never thought that five books later, with a small but loyal cult following of my alter ego, Lobo Solitario, my writing would develop into having lots of people praising me for their being able to live vicariously through my posts on social media, primarily Facebook. I am a sad social media user and if I added all the other platforms, I would eventually get lost myself as to what I posted and when. I am flattered that some people think my black and white work is similar to Ansel Adams. There is a huge growth as a photojournalist, poet and storyteller five books later. It's been interesting to see the production values get better with each book as well. Doing something you love doing eventually leads to success. The hard work and sacrifice occasionally lead to being rewarded by royalty checks, albeit in humbling amounts.

I found that with each book I'm now expecting a higher standard of photography, writing and production values. I had a nightmare situation, not realizing that I had apparently ordered book four, Noir et Blanc, on a non-glossy paper. The whole book, outside the glossy cover, was washed out. As I looked in shock at my author's copy, which I thought was my best book by far, I was distraught. To remedy the problem, I offered to send all those loyal customers my own personal files, which were true to the original book submitted. This still holds true today. I won't make that mistake again.

With eighty miles an hour being the new sixty-five miles speed limit of your favorite highway or interstate, my primary objective is how to be safe and stay upright no matter how short or long my day will be. My long, long days are limited to emergencies where "I have to get home and I'll just hoof it home" kind of day, averaging 450 miles a day for five days, when I'm east of the Mississippi River. It takes me a lot longer to recover physically from these days and the last time I did it, it took two days of recovery in my house, never leaving the yard.

These last two Haiku books have been produced in black and white and I'm now using a newer iPad. Although not the newest of the choices, I use the iPad 11.5 because of its size, with a keyboard, to take the pictures and organize the text. The technology of these new lenses can make most people look like a professional photographer. With buying new programs to enhance colors, I often wonder what the original picture would look like. I prefer to just see the shot as it is and discount a shot that looks too good to be true. The only reason that I have to use just one single black and white filter is because they don't make the iPad camera in a black and white lens.

I have often thought of those wonderful conversations I've had with small business owners in small towns off of two-lane roads looking for that Route 66 type diner with their blue-plate specials, career waitresses and homemade pies. For me, diners usually represent the town's cultural climate as you listen to the conversations while eating the Blue Plate Special.

There always seems to be the usual cast of characters like on Mayberry RFD, the family of four, mom and dad, with one rambunctious son and one freckled ponytailed daughter. Let's throw in a local businessperson, maybe owning a hardware and feed store and top it off with some hot shot dude wearing his baseball hat backwards, sporting rolled up short sleeves who races to a stop sign right in front of the diner in his all-metal muscle car. These descriptions might seem generalized but believe me, they still exist in rural America.

Another observation I have noted in my scratch paper, which I use for my notes from the day, is that in smaller towns in less populated areas, some locals have never left the state, county or even city they were born in. Wow. Imagine living fifty miles from baseball's famed Cooperstown, and never having been to the Baseball Hall of Fame if near Los Angeles, never going to Disneyland. Puzzling to say the least.

There have been times when I roll up to these eateries in a less announced manner. My ride kind of slithers in, not drawing much attention. They know I'm not a local and wonder why I am not riding a Harley. Then they may notice my eclectic looking Yamaha Super Tenere, with its twenty-seven pieces of yellow reflective tape on the windshield, amber running lights, and hand painted wolf on both sides of my 6.1-gallon gas tank. Everything seems safe until I'm heading for the counter, where I prefer to eat, and someone notices my California Bear patch on my jacket arm or proudly right above my heart.

I'm still confused about how people I've known for decades, who move away from the Golden State, spend a relatively noticeable amount of time on social media complaining about where they used to live. Gas prices, rent costs, and traffic are among their favorite topics. I'm sure there are some issues in their own state that they complain about as well and it's possible these people just like to complain.

After I post a provocative and dramatic picture, like a shot from Yosemite, I often mention "That's why I live in California." People are strangely extreme with their opinions of Californians and why people live there. We're living in such a polarized country, with extremists no longer flanking the ends of a Bell Curve at less than two percent, but whose numbers are more likely at least ten percent now. These are people you can't have a conversation within on almost any subject. They wonder why we have so many gay people, homelessness, so many drugs, divorces and rich people who don't pay any taxes. These people to me are obviously uninformed or just get a limited amount of material to make an informed decision regarding our cultural norms.

The one issue that always seems to come up is the border and immigrants. I shy away from most of this chat but occasionally I'll ask them if they like eating, going to restaurants or doing hard labor. The usual response refers to illegal drugs, corruption or believe it or not, "them people are taking away our jobs and raping our women." Yikes, really, you're kidding me, right? They don't get that without immigration, you would have no economy. The last time I checked, lots of Caucasian people aren't beating each other up to pick crops, wash dishes in restaurants or help slaughter animals in meat packing plants. I sometimes think that people are just envious of what California and the west coast has to offer. I'll always support and be a west coast supporter. I have no qualms about people who live elsewhere and hope they're happy where they are and let their negative comments die.

My assessment of this comes from the fact that a lot of the country seems not to have enough diversified information to form a decision that requires critical thinking, nor do they possess good listening skills. Not stupid, just not enough choices to have a calm conversation without using generalities or heaven forbid, "you must be a Democrat and a freakin' Liberal." If I could, I would eliminate the words conservative and liberal from the English language, along with woke, MAGA or whatever catch phrase of the time. What happened to just having a simple conversation, agreeing to disagree and then having a beer?

California is the country's most diverse and innovative state. From the early hula hoop days, surfing, beach parties and bikinis to today's electric cars, California is known for innovation and great foods, campgrounds, museums, draw dropping scenery and great year-round weather. (Excluding, of course, the occasional El Niña rainy seasons which produce destructive mudslides, earthquakes and lately more frequent and destructive fires that exact a heavy toll.)

I make no apologies for California's high cost of living standards. Forty million people later, I absolutely am disgusted by its traffic, lack of water conservation, obnoxious and demanding tourists, (who may be from your state) and people who feel entitled to whatever they want. That said, California has been home to me for 65 percent of my life, and I am now in my seventies. The other thirty five percent is in Portland, Oregon, or on the road.

I'm thankful I have my health and enough life experience and wisdom to navigate out of a lot of sticky situations. Don't get me wrong, most people are very helpful, curious and want to hear stories about your travels. They ask a lot of interesting questions, and I'm often asked to hang out or am invited to drop by their house the next time I'm passing through. But as I have mentioned, like my new interpretation of the Bell Curve, maybe at least ten to twelve percent of the country has a condition that I call "Rectumitis," a condition where people can't help themselves from being themselves, brought on by poor choices or possibly a shortage of equitable DNA.

That being said, enjoy the photos, Haikus and travelogs. I'll take care of the ride. (Sorry, I do text "Ha" a lot, so forgive me, as I need to make sure that some of my sarcasm is just that, sarcasm to make sure it's just that, funny.)

# Dry Docked

**Massive stainless steel  
Anomaly in the hood  
Years in the making**

*I often run into visual images that fascinate me. This one is in St. Johns, Portland, Oregon, in between an apartment complex and an industrial block. After noticing several security cameras as I circled (kind of stalked) the property, I caught the security guard's attention, and he was inside the building monitoring my movements. He didn't give out much info except it was a Verizon research center and it was privately owned by a family that had been randomly working on the boat for several years. After noticing the boat's porthole level, it wouldn't have been seaworthy anyway, as the portholes were below sea level.*

*Mark Fargo*

# Woman in Tree

Almost mermaid like
Your pose is enticing me
I can only hope

*The long, rainy and winter months engulf Oregon's landscapes with dense and vibrant green coats. The moss overwhelms the trees and rocks on the trail and makes rocks slippery in the streams. It's like an enchanted forest. This shot came along the thirty minute hike to Wilson Falls in the Tillamook State Forest.*

# Black Canyon Basement

Steep canyon-lined floor
Gunnison River green blue
reflective quiet

*Black Canyon National Park in Gunnison, Colorado, is famous for its sheer cliffs, painted walls and dark images. It doesn't get lots of sunlight because of its huge drops among the feldspar and mica mineral faces. It's a sixteen degree grade of serpentine paved road down to the river where I napped. The mouth of the watershed is on the Colorado River. Nearby is the Crystal Dam.*

*Mark Fargo*

# No White Cross

Nighttime blackness tomb
It's why they're called Badlands
Unmarked graveyard site

*Anza Borrego is California's largest state park, encompassing about 600,00 square acres. Designated a U.S. National Landmark in 1974, and named after 18th century Spanish explorer Juan Borrego, (a Spanish word meaning sheep), the park offers vibrant topographical landmarks throughout, ranging from flora and fauna, such as cactus, elephant trees, natural springs, oasis and the Famous Indian Head mountain. Kit foxes, road runners, golden eagles, and the list goes on. You'll need at least a week to experience this wonderland and see California's only native fan palm, pack a lunch and have a great outing.*

# Just Passing Through

Meandering roads
Smothering white clouds descend
Cooling the valley

*Depending on the time of year and location, while passing through these hovering blankets at higher altitudes, I can always count on a nervous nirvana. It's like the fog during the famous scene of the film "Casablanca." Low visibility while listening to my ride's guttural noise. Today I got to ride through these blankets, brief moments of anticipation and mystery - tomorrow, perhaps just the mountains' apex and elevation marker. Being on the road is a wonderful symbiotic relationship.*

*Mark Fargo*

# Single Parent of Two

Morning horizon
Close knit family
No neighbors seen here

*Somewhere between Brookings and Gold Beach, Oregon, this family of rocks reside in their own exclusive neighborhood. They don't travel much, never go on vacation, have their own private beach, don't mind the seasonal weather, eat together and use no technology, so they have never had the privilege of seeing TikTok. This family is very close, content and doesn't like change.*

# Alone But Not Lonely

**No signs of humans
two lane highways my first choice
cooling cloud cover**

*Some days on the road, while the air temp reaches in the nineties, the road temperature soars over a hundred degrees. Depending on the humidity you almost feel like you're in an oven. I often stop within an hour to hydrate and catch my breath. When the heavens send in cloud cover, I have even more respect for the road. Like I've said before, motorcycling is a privilege, not an entitlement.*

# Painted Wall

Sheer cliffs breathtaking
crystallized stone abstract art
hike at your own risk

*Western Colorado's Black Canyon National Park at Gunnison is the state's response to Arizona's big daddy Grand Canyon. It's not nearly as expansive as the Arizona site, but I would have to say the height and sheer drops in the Colorado park are overwhelmingly more intimidating. There's very little sunlight along the carved river flow. This wall reminds me of the painted hills, albeit less colorful, found in central Oregon's John Day National Fossil Beds Monument.*

# Fill in the Blanks

**More often than not
small town along the highway
missing some info**

*Depending on your sense of humor and/or political viewpoints, there are many ways to fill in the three missing letters on this sign. This gem was off Highway 217 in St. Francis, Kansas, a two-laner, my favorite type of road. I got many responses when I posted this on my last trip. Some humorous, some practical and one on the edgy side. Using your imagination, what would you have posted?*

*Mark Fargo*

# Restoring the Past

Madison County
covered bridges some damaged
wooden pegs no nails

*Madison County in Iowa is like other parts of America, known for its covered bridges. The movie with Clint Eastwood and Meryl Streep in 1995, "The Bridges of Madison County," made them even more visited. There are six bridges in the country and this one in particular, the Cedar Bridge, was vandalized in 2002 and later burned in 2017. The people of the town raised the money to rebuild and restore it, using the same type of wooden planks and wooden pegs for authenticity. Young love carvings remind us all of our youth.*

# Bones and Marrow

Filtered vibrant colors
walls on tracks for protection
flooding waters blocked

*I love these inclusive topography moments with our country's first mass transportation system, the railroad. Ironically, when the first locomotive blazed through the country coming out west, the first noticeable signs of what would be man's effect on the environment became apparent, especially to the Native Americans who couldn't understand the blackness spewing from the locomotive's stack.*

*Mark Fargo*

# Future Road Master

Determined game face
silos add to the background
she's ready to ride

*My ten year old granddaughter, Maya, is willing to try anything. When I asked her permission for this photo opportunity, she said "what time?" Being a farm-raised Iowa lass, where there are no rules for riding a motorcycle, hopped on right away. I suggested, though, that perhaps she needed a helmet to protect that beautiful face and hard-toe boots to shift gears.*

# Round Up

As promised went well
Even cockroaches missing
Nothing coming back

*So the community itself is left lifeless, no tenants nor businesses. A few service trucks use the area to leave their equipment between service jobs. Trying to understand if this was a billboard for a pesticide gone bad or just saying "Results Matter." Why not just say "Successful Test."*

# When It's Time

Challenging long days
twenty minutes does the job
Weeds asphalt rest stops

*As years pass by, my enthusiastic mind and aging body play games on one another. My mind tells me you can do a five hundred mile day if you leave at daybreak and eight to ten hours later, my mind tells me "Yeah, twenty years ago." Twenty years ago I wasn't even riding. I started riding at 60 and realized right away that a nap was in order, even traveling way fewer miles. On a motorcycle under blistering sunshine, chilly winds, four wheel texting assassins and sub-sixty temperatures, you take a beating. Above is an example of what my daily travels look like. Head on tank bag and any surface is welcomed.*

# Mile High

Game time sunny start
my Dodgers battling thin air
beating the weather

*It rarely happens that when I'm on the road I get a chance to see a baseball game. My visit to my nephews' house in Aurora, Colorado, gave me a slim window to catch a game and a stadium I've never been to, Coors Field. A mile high beautiful venue and a great seat. Very warm day turned into thunder showers and rain by the 9th inning. Loved it when the lights came on to this view. Dodgers won 5-3.*

*Mark Fargo*

# The Strong Silent Type

My cousin talking
without speaking how he feels
lots of us nodding

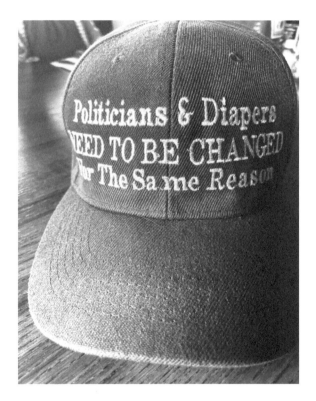

*It's not unusual for me to run into people all over the country who, like the T-shirts they wear, are expressing themselves or identifying enjoyment without talking. Our current political climate is toxic and unproductive. Walk softly and carry a big hat so to speak. Can't tell if he is pro-donkey or pro-elephant. This hat is telling me he is not happy with either choice coming in November of 2024. Maybe he isn't voting this time.*

# Sandy Extinction

**No tarpits nearby
climate and hunting their fate
passed among the dunes**

*As a lone rider, photographer and writer, I often see objects, or might I say, subjects, in a different light. I automatically saw this wooden Mojave resident as a Woolly Mammoth casualty. I discovered this in the Kelso Dunes while I was looking to photograph something else. That's the beauty of desert communities, you have your tourists' recommendations of places to see, but often I find other stunning results.*

## Desert Bloom

Winter flowering
short lifespan in the desert
rain its caregiver

*Anza-Borrego State Park is the largest state park in California, with reportedly close to 700,000 acres. It has its Badlands, unique mineral deposits and alluvial fans like many other desert communities, but it also offers a wide variety of colorful seasonal cactus blooms, depending on the rainy season, of course. The bighorn sheep get a special perk there as a large portion of the park is closed from June 1st until September 30th for their watering needs in the rest of the park. Not unusual to see them on the golf course, without tee times.*

# Short Stack?

**Frisbee like Bisquick
could feed family of four
I was one and done**

*Oftentimes when I'm on the road, I camp. The campground office staff usually provide a simple breakfast like biscuits and gravy, scrambled eggs and pancakes. This campground, just outside the already-booked-months-ahead in the Badlands in South Dakota, was no exception. I had a horrendous tent camping experience the night before, with no sleep, and I almost went into a coma when I saw these. They dwarfed the paper plate they came on. Could easily feed a family of four, unless you have teenagers.*

*Mark Fargo*

# Perspective

Today's new tractor
half million and change
no license needed

*Industry leading John Deere's latest all-purpose vehicle is impressive, to say the least. Didn't get to see the inside technology-friendly interior, but I imagine you could order lunch from the console, delivered, of course, as ordering to-go would be asking too much at any drive-up window.*

# Rough Terrain

Settled in stillness
high interfluves sharp ravines
native sacred sites

*The Badlands of South Dakota are like many other badlands in other national parks. Desolate, sharp rocks to navigate, local tundra and species that thrive in their environment. The black-footed ferret, one of the world's most endangered species, has been reintroduced here. Always have the right gear to explore these conditions or find yourself with self-inflicted wounds at day's end.*

*Mark Fargo*

# Stuck Forever

Extinct species now
the fish that didn't get away
mudstone was his grave

*The Badlands in South Dakota is a pretty harsh reality for the species that live there. Perhaps many hundreds of thousand a of years ago fish were dinosaur-like in size and faced many challenges. Over time we discover their remains, such as this fish gasping for its last breath of air.*

# Sky Blankets

Darkened puffy piles
man made pathway for my ride
woven masterpiece

*There are times, just from the highway itself, that provide me with brilliant images of solo highway travel. I just get off my bike and take it all in. I can shoot landscapes all day long after brief hikes and navigating down hills for better angles and perspectives. There's lots of opportunity when you get off the interstates to roads less traveled. I chose this for my book cover because all of my literary works contain a road on the cover.*

*Mark Fargo*

## Please Come Back

Your brilliant orange coat
milkweed your favorite meal
transparent beauty

*California and Mexico, your winter homes, provide the needed heat for your enabling body temperatures that allow flight and appropriate roosting vegetation for your vacation needs. Sumacs, elm, willow and other indigenous trees provide cover from robins, sparrows, mice and Asian Lady Beetles, to name just a few.*

# Time Out

**No carnage this beach
tis the season for mating
tis the time for rest**

*Piedras Blancas Seal Elephant Rookery is a well-visited tourist spot up along the central coast of California near Morro Bay. Best viewing spots year round are about five miles north of Hearst Castle. You might need ear plugs as the bulls are battling for their mates, pups are searching for moms and the beach gets more crowded than Highway 101. Quite entertaining for everyone.*

*Mark Fargo*

## Limited Hours

Daily six to eight
local problems are discussed
news spreads very fast

*I've seen literally over a hundred of these on my travels. Rural places with limited population, limited hours and the building next to them, here pictured on the right, the previous post office. One of my nephews wife is the Post Master General, working for seventeen dollars an hour, two hours a day, six days a week. She knows everybody in town. Old building to the right, has a tenant now in the dilapidated remains.*

# It's Quiet Time

**Tides out tide pools in
from the dunes the sun settles
framed by tall grasses**

*The condensed Oregon coastline, three hundred and forty two miles of it, about five hundred miles less than the 30 plus sunblock sandy beaches of southern California. It is more rugged in some areas, home to many solo rocks, driftwood and families and their dogs. Beach towns here, like in Manzanita, Oregon, are flooded with unique businesses, a variety of restaurants and local charm. A great way to escape the heat.*

*Mark Fargo*

# The GHOAT

No grazing today
Brady got nothing on you
known for his kindness

*My partner of twenty-four years, Maggie Mary Morrison, her five other siblings and lots of relatives and well wishers got to spend three days celebrating John Morrison's 100th birthday in July of 2024. A twenty-year Air Force lieutenant colonel veteran who served in four wars, worked as a counselor at Juvenile Hall, and was an Oregon high school state wrestling champion, he is still amazing. He's still as sprite as ever, lives by himself and frequently walks the neighborhood and greets everybody he meets. The celebration included nine holes of golf in between the dinner boat river cruise and well attended sausage BBQ with many well wishers. He was a wonderful husband of sixty seven years to Margaret, his wife who passed six years earlier, a father, grandfather and great grandfather, living by himself in town and enjoying lots of attention from everybody, including myself. We lunch occasionally, discuss politics and sports and afterwards have See's candies for dessert. Yum.*

## Road Traveled (in case I'm not around)

Tens of thousands of miles
days....weeks.... months....years now passed
white mane....white mustache....white stubble now
butt soft as my custom made seat

thousands of searing sunsets
chilly early morning sunrises afternoon weed naps
my body struggling eastern morning glare
empty stomach achy body start my day

silenced two lane highways wheat fields
sunny shadowless mountain serpentine roads favorites
out of nowhere monsoon deluges....slight smile no shelter
diners....cheap motels....tent areas with grass and shade

buzzards circling my arrival earth cracking desert zones
indigenous inhabitants not surviving the night
smelled some though never seen
hitchhikers sorry....no room

rainbow of people met best at heart
some unhappy jealous desolate anti California chimes
befriended some shared meals finding common ground
back on the road next day

many stray dogs witnessed
angry they've been abandoned
sense their distrust
eventually come over to feed drink water

images I'll never forget
my photos my Haiku my memories
regretful few conversations
human nature its worst its best

lone wolf my soul's deep heartfelt mate
never worried about time route or destination
never worried about death
smiling at keys final turn left.....no regrets

## PAVEMENT PROTECTOR

My Mandalorian style helmet, with electrical tape added to block glare and narrow my scanning vision, protects me from road hazards and other four wheeled vehicles of various shapes and sizes.

## Author's Notes

Most of my close friends are becoming concerned about my life on the road now that our lifelong friends are in our seventies. Hell, some wanted to know why I was even thinking of riding a motorcycle. Their concern, I believe, is mostly because of the lack of enforcement on today's roads and some leaders in this country, especially politicians, who basically say it's okay to break laws because it's your constitutional right to break them. Yea right. We all have observed that many car drivers are distracted by technology, eating, kissing and singing along to their favorite music. Throw in speed with no-look lane changes and you have a recipe for fatalities. I have met career riders who have never been hit, but self-crashed from fatigue or just being unlucky, like when they hit gravel. I hope I join the elite club of survivors as I leave the road.

California has decided that there are too many motorcycle fatalities in the under-thirty and post-sixty age groups. Instead of rewarding those who have no tickets or points on their record, they have decided to create an almost unpassable written test to renew your license. This coming from a state that was the first to allow lane-splitting for motorcyclists between cars in congested traffic, so you don't have fifty bikers in a single file behind other cars, creating an enormous backlog of crawling cars or stopped traffic. The DMV has yet to say if these accidents are car-related or just reckless behavior from these two age groups.

Perhaps at print time for Bone and Marrow I will finally pass this test which is set for failure regardless of your knowledge and skills. When you renew your bike license you also have to pass the written test for your car. I never studied for the car exam; I haven't owned a car for over seven years but miraculously have passed the car exam with no problems. What's this say about the DMV 's fairness in their testing protocol? To date I haven't passed the written test, but the DMV gladly holds out their hand for my forty-one dollar renewal fee without batting an eye. You get three chances to pass each time. With highlighting and several hours of study, no luck yet, but at least I can get a three-month extension in between test failures. It's getting expensive.

I've had two friends my age, smart men with tons of experience, just stop riding, noting that the test wasn't based on practical common-sense riding, but created for failure, not knowledge of the rules of the road. BTW, it took me 15 tries to pass the M1 and class C test simultaneously. A Guinness Book record perhaps, but with only one point (I got squeezed by a car when I was lane-splitting at ten miles an hour) and no tickets with over 200,000 miles on my record, I wasn't about to give up my passion for the road. The test has since been modified as the multiple algorithms of confusing questions produced too many people failing multiple times.

I've personally been targeted a few times on the pavement because people have no regard for life and have no self-respect. There is just something wrong with their thinking or possibly they have such turmoil in their lives, or they just don't care. I am constantly scanning in a 180-degree horizontal plane and checking my side view mirrors. I feel very confident in my capabilities to escape danger, but at no time do I feel entitled out there. It is a privilege to be able to be on that road on two wheels. It's a nirvana like nothing else.

One more hazardous factor is, of course, being under twenty-five years old with no fear of anything with a "it just can't happen to me" mentality, lack of fear at any speed, driving drunk or high on drugs. I never think I am a Marvel comic superhero. I respect the road and feel privileged to be able to ride everyday if I choose to and feel blessed that my health is good and I'm mentally in a good space. There is a lot of resentment as well about California's lane splitting law that allows motorcyclists to drive in between cars when traffic is slow and to move up further into the pack. There are almost one million registered motorcyclists in California, more than the populations of Wyoming, Alaska, North Dakota and Vermont and the District of Columbia. Some of that resentment is deserved, as the riders with fewer fairings (i.e., less bulk) are bolting in between cars at the legal speed limit, instead of a more reasonable speed of let's say, twenty-five to thirty miles an hour. Other states will probably adopt this policy or something similar out of political pressure down the road. Gee, another innovative idea from California that has lots of support and just as much hatred.

I find some people who hold Californians accountable for their driving may never have had the pleasure of driving in some southern states like Tennessee. I find the whole Volunteer state as one big NASCAR raceway. If everybody's going the speed limit that means you should add ten plus miles to that posted speed. Even in the slow lanes, where I hang out on some Interstates, it's not uncommon to see someone on my tail ten feet away going seventy miles per hour, wondering why I'm not going ten plus more per hour in the slow lane as well.

I also notice that a lot of cars in Tennessee are not your usual just off the lot stock styles. Added chrome, tinted windows, and pinstripes are the norm as well as running lights of all sizes and colors. It's kind of like the Harley Davidsons on four wheels type of state. Yes, that would include the usual number of pickups with American or Confederate flags proudly streaming from the tailgate section, or

American flag license plate frames over the license. Like I've said before, this country is made up of fifty different cultures.

I'm also in the process of revamping all my Motorcycle Haiku books to a glossy format paper and revamping my website as well. It's especially effective for black and white copy. I'm constantly trying to make improvements for your access to my travels, poetry and purpose for sharing my life and vision. It's been an enlightening experience for me and my growth as a person has been unmatched in my previous sixty years.

In my five Motorcycle Haiku books I've talked about many motorcycle-related subjects like the frequently discussed helmet versus no helmet laws, (if you're a donor I'm not sure I care), entitlement and privilege for being on the road and why people ride the bikes they ride, just to name a few. I've also expressed my concerns for the empathetic human condition, which I feel hasn't changed much over time, but it does seem more common among the masses now to feel more neglected, misrepresented and looked down upon. There is a wide distribution of wealth for the "haves" in this country and much less wealth available for the "have nots" despite the country's economic successes. Wall Street is about making money, not making America equitable for all. It's like Las Vegas, the house always wins.

I wish we were back to being a purple country and people could respect one another's opinions without such discourse. I hope in my lifetime our country returns to one standard deviation from the Bell Curve mean, politically and financially. I know I'm a dreamer, but I'm okay knowing when I leave this place, I left it better than when I started.